FROM
FEAR
TO
FAITH

BARBARA HARRIS

outskirtspress
DENVER, COLORADO

Outskirts Press, Inc.
http://www.outskirtspress.com

ISBN: 978-1-4787-6216-4

Outskirts Press and the "OP" logo are trademarks belonging to Outskirts Press, Inc.

PRINTED IN THE UNITED STATES OF AMERICA

Dedication

This book is dedicated to my mother, Mary Lou Harris; my sister, Nancy Bailey, and her husband, David; to God and Christ and all of my angels including by beloved friends

"The Swing of Life"

Life is funny in many ways

It's like a swing that continually sways

Sometimes it seems we're up so high

That we could reach and touch the sky

And then at times it swings so low

We wear a smile so no one knows

Barbara Harris

Foreword

This book was an inspiration given to the author by others. Whilst writing, she found strength, hope and peace to go on. It was from inspiration from those who have gone on before her. Challenged by love, it was created to bring hope and peace of mind to others.

It is a story of a woman who had no hope at all. At the age of 48, she found the power within to recover from drugs, alcohol and many mental diseases. Now a useful member of society, she has dedicated her life to helping others.

Her prize for this new life is freedom. Freedom from bondage of self and self-will. It is an inspiring tale that contains suggestions that may help others. It is a presentation of how life could be better for those suffering from mental disease and destruction from drugs and alcohol.

It depicts an example of a life that allows her spirituality and love to help others. Simple charm, grace, and the support from others make her life an example.

Table of Contents

CHAPTER 1

Childhood

I live on Rossell Street and there are witches in my bedroom closet. I could see them. This made me feel very afraid and catatonic. I went into the fetal position for protection. This was the first clue that there was something wrong with me. I knew no one else could see or hear these witches. I saw the witches and watched them fly around the closet on brooms. I got very scared. I called out to Nancy, my sister…she was asleep. I woke her up and told her there were witches in the closet and asked if I could sleep next to her. The morning came and I was safe. It seemed my whole life from that point on revolved around staying safe. I was always afraid of something. I never knew what. I never wanted to be alone for long after that. The early stages of schizophrenia had set in.

It was not until I was in alcohol recovery that I knew why I was dying in pain. I knew I always got real high and very low. I imagined a lot of things. I was distant from everyone. Ironically enough, I was always very out-going and friendly and could make friends easily. I never felt equal to anyone inside. I always felt I was unusual. I had a lot of pride and indignation for anyone who could act normal. I never died so to speak, but boy, did I want to. I never knew why. At the age of 48, I got into recovery and as the alcohol obsession was lifted; I was diagnosed with manic depression (rapid cycling), schizophrenia and panic disorder. It took a lot of self-discerning over my entire life to accept this diagnosis. I had to reflect on my life and all the odd things that I had seen, heard and experienced, asking questions to other mentally ill people to see if they had experienced such things. I finally decided I was sick. I could fake it so well that no one knew I went into a three year depression. I was always faking it and can remember this voice from an invisible person always telling me I am unusual when it felt like I was acting or feeling funny. It was as if it was supporting me in my actions. Always reassuring me that what I was doing was okay. Later I found out this was my Spirit Guide, Virgil. Always finding the pain inside me, I would just go on about my day like nothing unusual was happening.

Here is an account of what happened in my life…some of the joys and many of its sorrows. I now continue to turn my life around to help those who also suffer not only from addiction and mental disorders, but also from displeasing and stressful events caused by disease in their lives.

It is now years since I turned to Christ and God for the answers. Many miracles have happened to me in these nineteen years. Later in the book I will share them with you.

The Christmas Eve before I was born, my father bought the new baby a football. He wanted a baby boy. Without concern, he bought Christmas tree lights and a new football for the new baby that night. I was born two days later, and surprise, I was a girl. He never forgot that night as he never got a son, but boy did he have a lot to handle with me.

When I was five, I went to a strawberry field next to my house and found God there. While eating a strawberry, I looked up and found my whole heart full of love and the bible told me that was God. I ate the strawberry fast and said to Him, "I love you, God, thank you very much for explaining yourself to me." I never forgot that experience. It is still with me.

I went on many trips with my parents and sister and I always felt isolated or disturbed. I could never feel comfortable. One time, while riding in the car, I was having trouble with sitting still and this voice came to me and said, "Christ will always be with you." I did not mention this to anyone, but it gave me a lot of comfort. It relieved me of a lot of fear.

One of the flowers in the Nutcracker Suite when I was seven

I had a real normal childhood. Christmastime was my greatest memory. My sister and I usually got everything we wanted ... but we knew not to ask for anything too extravagant.

One time, when we were really young, Nancy and I had gotten matching red velvet dresses for Christmas. Not long after that, the family went out to dinner and I noticed Nancy was drinking the cream out of the tiny bottles on the table. We were wearing our matching red dresses, I decided I wanted to try that too, but I spilled mine all over my new red dress. Boy, did I get it! I got spanked so hard when we got home that even Nancy cried. That made me feel real good; I knew she knew what I was going through. She actually came over and sat with me after things were over and told me everything would be all right.

Nancy has always been a guardian angel in my life. I do not know what I would have done without her. My dad was another fond memory of mine. When he held me on his lap I could have hugged him for hours and I knew I was safe and that he understood. He was a wonderful father and always let Nancy and me play with him. One time we told him to come into the kitchen after we finished the dishes. We asked him to put his bald head down. He did. Then we tapped the clean pots on his head telling him that they were as shiny as his bald head. We all laughed and he got a real kick out of that. I loved my father.

Another fond memory of my father was his birthdays. His birthday was on April Fools' Day. Each and every year we played a trick on him. It was a ritual with us. One year we decorated this cardboard cake and put it over his real birthday cake. The cardboard cake looked exactly like a real cake. The knife was handy but when he tried to cut the cake, he realized that it was a fake cake. We all spread good cheer and when he laughed we all said, "April Fool's". Another time we surprised him with a "garlic box". My father hated everything about garlic. We mashed about four or five cloves in a tiny box lined with cotton. We wrapped it and put it in a bigger box. We then wrapped the bigger box and put that in a still bigger box. We wrapped that box until we had a huge present for him to open. He opened every package and got a dose of the garlic box and smelled it, he then said, "Yuk!".

As a child, I noticed I was always getting in trouble. One time I was sitting on a footstool, learning how to write with a ballpoint pen and I drew three concentric circles on the brand new wall-to-wall carpet. My mother got furious and beat me with a brush and hanger. I was pushed up against a coral rock planter and scratched my leg. My legs still have the scars from that planter. I was sent to my room and had to wait for my father to come home. When he got home, he spanked me with an elastic stretch belt. I remember faking the crying because the elastic belt did not really hurt. I was just glad when he had left my room.

I was about eight years old and while visiting relatives all the older children in the house got to go see the movie "Psycho". Nancy and I always wanted to go to with them but everyone said it would bother me too much. I never was diagnosed with mental disease as a child, or teenager so I didn't know the effect this movie would have on me. I returned home and went to see this movie with a childhood friend. I was nuts for about six weeks. No one knew what was bothering me because I couldn't tell them. I had to sneak out to see it, and would get into real trouble if found out. My mental disease manifested in an over-active imagination.

Then there was the time I hit my sister with the hose. We were asked to clean up the yard. I was rolling the garden house when Nancy and I got into a fight. I aimed the nozzle at her and hit her to the right of her nose. I did not know it would hurt her. Nancy started yelling. My mom came running out of the house to see what happened and there I was holding the hose, with nozzle dangling, and Nancy's nose bleeding. "She hit me in the nose with that," she said. I was in trouble again and was sent to my room for punishment. I never figured out why Nancy always got the benefit of the doubt because I did not think I had done anything wrong. Anyway, she had started it! I think Nancy still has a scar on her nose from this. My hyper activeness from a manic high was in full force. With manic depressive thinking, you always think you are right when, in reality, you are wrong because your perception of the sequence of how things actually happen is wrong. The manic depressive person only perceives what he sees and, without proper medication, he usually comes off saying he is right and doesn't understand why everyone is against him. It is brutal for him as it makes the pain worse and he usually feels he has been rejected and mistreated.

Another time, my mother and Aunt Amelia came home from a luncheon and I had gotten most of the neighborhood kids up on the roof playing. I had everyone climb up the vine holder to the roof. We were having a ball. We were playing "Go!" We ran to any place on the roof that was safe. We kept doing this and none of us wanted to come down. Finally, my mom whistled from the back yard with one of her loud clear whistles. WE ALL STOPPED. Then I heard it, "Barbara, are you up there" "Yeah, Mom, I am up here, what do you want?" "I want you to come down immediately." I noticed there was impatience in her voice. I climbed down the vine holder and said, "What's up?" She said, "Stay down here and tell the children to come down and go home." "Okay", I said. My manic depression was on again. I got one of my crazy wild ideas and it was a success. I had gotten all the kids up there and we were having fun. Crazy kind of fun, that's what I liked. I had won and gotten all the people back that had told me I had been wrong in the past. We did not have any serious talk or anything, but I think my mother knew something was wrong with me.

Not long after that I was taken to a doctor for my hyperactive behavior. He wanted Mom to put me on tranquillizers. Mom just could not do this because she believed I was just being a child. She has been such a good mom. No one could match her as she was always doing for me. She is now deceased. Her strength has inspired in me a great serenity, peacefulness and the love of mankind

CHAPTER 2

The Early Days

My drinking started at an early age. Mom and Dad would have great parties. After the guests left, I would drink up all the half-finished drinks. The stuff tasted good and I thought I was being "cool" to drink like the grown-ups. The drinks were great, kind of funny on the stomach, but I liked them.

We moved from Chicago to Miami when I was five years old. It was a nice move. Mom cried the whole way as she was leaving her family up north. Dad had asthma and the doctors said he would be better in a warmer climate. My aunt (father's sister) and her husband had already moved down there from Chicago. They were living in Coral Gables. So we joined them and I started working for my uncle's car dealership. We moved into a house on Alhambra Circle right across from the University of Miami. There was a football field next door to the ROTC Building where I used to play. This was the house I grew up in until I entered high school.

One day I was playing with this girl who lived down the street. Suddenly she stood up and hit me with a crowbar in the stomach. I did not know what to do. She screamed, "You are fat!" I was horrified for I always feared my weight would be a problem in life. I started crying and ran home as fast as I could. I could hear my mom whistling for me to come home for dinner.

I was relieved to hear that whistle. This time, it meant home and safety. I told my mom what happened. I was still crying hysterically. My stomach hurt. Mom quieted me down. I had dinner. I remember feeling different after that. I was a lot quieter. I held things inside more and kept secrets in my heart. I had been defenseless and I was attacked. My weight issue had always been a problem for me. I had feelings of loneliness and isolation after that. Mom told me that I was never the same after that. My psychiatrist and I have discussed this incident and we wonder whether this wasn't the start of my manic depression and some of my mental problems. I started feeling like a victim.

One of my favorite childhood things

When I was an infant, our nurse, Mac, put sugar in my milk to make me stop crying. She said it worked real well. Still today I experience cravings for sweets and sugar, which alter my mood. This is not too hard to understand. Sugar today, in many kids, is a mood altering substance. Usually it is a stimulator and makes children hyper. With me it was the opposite. It made me feel sedated and calm. Today sometimes I have to eat an ice cream bar before I go to bed to sedate me and bring my hyper manic mind down. I think I inherited the genes for manic depression. The sugar Mac gave me calmed my senses.

Drinking caffeine definitely affects the manic depression and its highs and lows. Once I got the picture of this, I quit drinking caffeine. Water was the best replacement for me. It helps keep me balanced and stabilized and makes me feel much better. Decaffeinated drinks are also a good replacement. This little girl named Lilly, a daughter of a friend of mine, started praying for me to quit drinking diet cokes. I was hooked on them. I thought I never could get off of them. But then I felt these prayers from her and the change to drink water came easily. Just the thought of this little child praying for me really touched my heart. Ever since I got into recovery I can feel prayers. It is an amazing thing. Sometimes I can even feel whose prayers are coming from whom.

In Junior High I cheated on a test. The class was English Grammar. I expected I was going to have trouble on this spelling test, so I wrote all the words down with ink on the desk. After I was done, I turned the paper into the teacher. When I was leaving the classroom, I noticed she was checking the tops of the desk for writing. I raced down the hall to leave the building and I heard someone calling my name. They said that I was in trouble and to report back to the classroom. I deliberately lied for I was put on the spot. I did not know what to tell her. Finally, I gave up and told her the truth that I had done it. I was escorted to detention. After that I went home and told no one. I never did that again, cheat on a test.

Ponce de Leon Junior High School

Award of Honor

presented to

BARBARA HARRIS

in appreciation of special service rendered and in recognition of unselfish contribution of time and effort.

Joanne M. Boyden
Instructor
PONCE
Student Council

J. J. Norton
Principal

Award of Honor in Junior High School

I won a car the summer after my junior year in high school. I picked Nancy up from work. She was going to a debutante ball that night and was in a hurry. The WQAM mustang, Channel 5.6 AM, was behind us and we were listening to them on the radio. Then this amazing thing happened. They described our license plate number and model of our car and told us to pull over. Nancy did not want to do this because she was running late, but I insisted and she said yes. When she pulled over, I jumped out of the car and my name was placed in the drawing of about twenty thousand and they gave me this great radio.

I knew I was going to win this drawing for a 1965 mustang. I never told anyone.

About two months later I listened for the drawing announcement. The day of the drawing I went dress shopping with Mom and to the beach with friends. Everyone was teasing me about winning that Mustang. I finally gave in and told everyone I was going to win. Later that night, about 5 pm, the announcement was going to be made. I prayed to God that someone less fortunate than me, might win the Mustang, then sell it and get a new lease on life.

Finally, the drawing time was here. When they read out my name and address I jumped for joy and kept yelling "I Won, I Won, and I Won." I wrote down the phone number on the dresser with an eyebrow pencil. My mom came in and thought I was screaming because she thought Nancy had gotten in a boat accident. Finally she shook me - I screamed, "I won the WQAM mustang on the radio and I only have fifty-six seconds to call in!" "Let's run to the kitchen where both lines are, I'll call information and you dial the number to the station on the second line!" We did just that.

I got in on the fifty-fifth second. They said I had won. I couldn't believe it. Little did I know they were taping my response, "Oh, I don't believe it, I won. I won, I won!!! I think I am going to faint." This was such a "smashing" tape that they played it over and over again on the radio for a month until I picked up the car.

I had my choice of any and every option I wanted on the car. I ordered it "fully loaded" in royal blue with white interior and white convertible top, air conditioning and four-on-the-floor!!!!! I was so excited!!!!!!! I couldn't wait to pick it up. For a month, I had to listen to the tape they made of me. I was so embarrassed. Finally, the day to pick up the car was here. The first time I saw it I couldn't believe it was so beautiful. It was a royal blue Ford Mustang - Four-on-the-floor, air conditioned with a white convertible top. It was a lean machine and I couldn't believe it was mine!

I didn't know how to drive a four-on-the-floor. A crowd was gathered. Finally, I got to get in the car. Nancy was in the passenger seat. She had a coke in her hand and I told she had better not spill it all over the new white interior or I would kill her. We chugged and plugged our way out of the parking lot. I stalled two to three times until I could get the right gears and the clutch. Finally, I got it and off we went - driving everywhere and so excited to love a car like this. I never forgot that prayer I said before they drew my name. And I still feel that winning that car was a gift from God for my obedience to Him.

The summer before this, Mom said I could have a party for all my friends. We invited everyone. I think there was some drinking going around but I didn't partake because Mom was in the family room and she would get mad at me. I hid my drinking from my parents. One friend of mine, Johnny threw Richard's hat into the pool. Richard jumped and didn't see that the sliding glass door was closed. He walked right through it. In any event, everybody stopped. Richard was okay except for his forehead, which needed a few stitches. We took him to the Emergency Room. He was fine when he got back to the party. Believe it or not, my mom didn't freak out.

1964 Coral Gables Senior High

In High School I was a member in good standing of the sorority, Co-Eds. I was elected Vice-President in my junior year. We did a lot of fun things; like raising money by selling donut holes from house to house, car washes, etc. There were a lot of other clubs like ours in my high school, but Co-Eds was the most fun and genuine. We did some not so "cool" things too. Much to our parent's dismay, we would soap the fountains and laughed about how they looked to people the next day. I was a leader of the pack at this. We also toilet papered trees in the front yards of friends' houses, just for a joke. We also threw raw eggs on peoples' houses and cars just for fun. It was called "egging".

Now that I am a homeowner, I look back on this and see what a waste it was. Then, whippersnapper me, took some friends up to the University of Miami's Medical School's morgue and showed them the cadavers that were stored there. We couldn't stand the "stench" and got the heebie-jeebies and left real quickly. There were too many dead corpses there for us to handle. I was always in Honor Classes and made good grades, however, my conduct out of class was not as acceptable. Life was good to me.

At this time, we were living in the guest house down the street from my uncle's home. This was the house that my sister's husband grew up in. When they finally got married, Nancy was living in the bedroom that he grew up in. There were many funny stories that came from that house. Only one of them comes to mind now. Nancy and I were in the house alone and I opened the linen closet door and a big flying cockroach came out. I screamed. Nancy came running and found me dodging and running from this cockroach all around the living room. It wouldn't leave me alone. I was desperate. Finally, still screaming, I ran out to the front porch and it slowly left my collar. That was a long, long time for a cockroach to be on your collar.

With all this fun going on, my father announced that we would be moving to West Palm Beach. He had acquire a new job and told us we all had to move. I did not like this, as it was my senior year and I, like most kids my age, wanted to graduate with all my best friends and party all year round. This was most depressing to me and, even though I had a new mustang to go back and forth to Miami each weekend, it just wasn't the same.

I couldn't accept it and I pouted and moped the first six months in

West Palm Beach. It really was ridiculous, moving my senior year. I hated studying, or being in family functions. I disliked everything in my life except my car; sister and my friends back home. Towards the middle of the year, I came out of my depression und began acting normal again. I got accepted at the University of Florida and that really made me alive again.

CHAPTER 3
My Father's Suicide

During my senior year in West Palm, we built a beautiful home on the Inter-coastal Waterway. This began to bring the family back together. We had a lot of fun in that house. Living on the water made the house really calm and beautiful. It seemed Mom cooked the best meals she ever did in that house. We all became friends as a family.

Then evil took us by surprise. My dad was fired from his job. We all cried. We were such a close family. It seemed my dad had gotten so much credit for the accomplishments he made in the local car industry that one of his bosses got jealous and had my dad fired.

My dad didn't know what to do. Here he had moved the whole family up here, built a new house, had two daughters in college, and no money and no job. As you can imagine he was very upset. Finally he found a used car dealership that he could afford. He ran it beautifully to every detail. My mom helped. But it was not like a new car dealership with all the excitement, clamor and trimmings.

Because of this, my father encountered financial difficulties so I gave him the new car I had won to pay off the taxes on his used car dealership. The year 1967 was one of disaster! I remember walking through a field on campus thinking this Thanksgiving would be the first time the family would be together. My father had been sick. Mom wouldn't tell me what was the matter with him.

He got very depressed. We were all so worried about him. Finally he became sick and could not leave the house. This was so sad. I came home one weekend unexpectedly from school to cheer him up. I brought him some ice cream one afternoon. He told me to sit down; he had something he wanted to tell me. "What's up, Dad?" "I know that whatever you do, you will do a good job of it," he said. I didn't know why he had said this, but I did know I would remember it for the rest of my life.

On November 6, 1967, my father committed suicide. He waited until Mom's sister and brother were in the house, so Mom wouldn't be alone. He planned the whole thing, right down to a file with all the current papers we would need. We were now a family of three. My sister was already working her first job after college. I was in my sophomore year in college. The house was full of relatives by the time I got home from school. No one would tell me how my dad died. My mom wouldn't, my sister wouldn't, and my aunt wouldn't. Finally I locked myself in the den and demanded to know how he died. Finally, mom came in. I could tell she was full of fear and fright. Finally she told me he had killed himself. I let out a scream so loud that God heard it and sent my aunt and grandmother running into the room. I said, "No, no, he couldn't have. He taught me about God. And God doesn't do that. What's worse, he didn't live up to his word." "He was sick, darling.", mom said.

The funeral was terrible. I had never been to a funeral. The casket was closed. He had shot himself in the head while in the shower. My mom found him dead on the floor in pools of blood. I never will forget the picture my mom must have seen when she found him. My poor mom, I never knew how she got over that sight. I guess he must have felt he failed us as a family and was having very severe financial difficulties. I never thought my father would ever do a stunt like this. He was a man of the church and very well looked upon by family and community. He killed us all. When he died, we died. The family unit, my mother made sure that didn't happen. But a part of all of us died with him. He was a very good man. He never let me nor my sister or mom down. He just disappeared forever. I was thinking all this during the funeral. I was very upset and angry, but I hid it all. Warmth came from my sister again as she knew how I felt.

The final straw came a day or two later. I told my mom I wanted to stay out of school for the rest of the trimester. I was too afraid of facing the peer group back at the sorority house where I lived. I begged her. I wanted to stay at home with family until I got over the death. My mom said, "No, your father would have had a fit." "You have to go back to college." I thought that was cruel.

So back to college I went. Well, what a depression set in. I just couldn't fight it. Plus I was angrier then hector at my father and least, but not last, God, my old faithful provider. It came to "Do I take drugs to get over this or suffer in depression for a real long time". My manic depression really set in. There were highs and then there were lows. I couldn't stand the pain so I bought some pot from this friend and stored it in my closet at the sorority house. Every night I went over to my friend's house and smoked pot. I stayed high a lot and it helped me to get over the pain.

Then one day, my roommate, who was president of the sorority, asked me if I was smoking pot. I said no. She said my name was on a list with three others in the house that were suspected of smoking marijuana. They lifted my pin along with three other girls in the house. We were expelled for smoking pot. I was Chaplain of the sorority at this time.

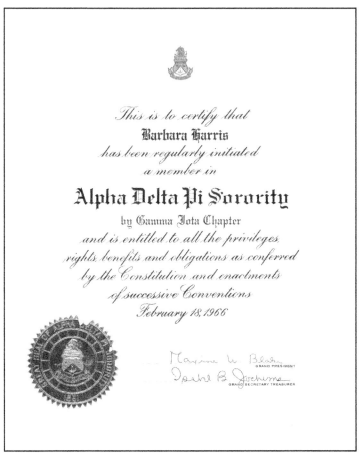

Sorority Certificate

My mom defended me to the House Mother because I was a good kid and had done so much for the sorority; but their system came down on me. I did not have the heart to tell my mom the truth - that I had done drugs. I was too afraid it would hurt her. I moved into on-campus housing the last trimester of my senior year. I felt so alone, so bare, and so desolate. Another depression set in. Once again, I felt like a victim.

Somehow, I managed to graduate from the University of Florida with good grades in my major Marketing/Advertising/Communications. I aced all my finals. One of my most favorite stories of my freshman year happened when I was majoring in Interior Design. I had this Oriental professor who taught 101 Drawing. He was such a hard teacher, we called him "Mr. Parallel Lines." My classes were at 7:30AM. I could barely "see" during these classes let alone draw anything creative. Mornings are bad for the manic depressive person and this interfered with my performance in this class.

We had to draw a picture in scale of some famous person for our final project. I chose Vincent Van Gogh and finished the project by staying up all night. The next day I turned it in with pride and took off to Daytona Beach for the weekend. On Monday morning I went to my drawing class and the professor wanted to see me after class. I went to see him, and he thought my roommate, Linda, majoring in Fine Arts, had done my final project. I almost died. I kept telling him no, that I had done it and he insisted that this was "A" work and that my class work was always "C" and that he didn't think I could do such good work. I walked out of his office so angry that I decided to change majors. I got a "C" in this class. I did change my major. I wanted to stay with a creative major; marketing major advertising as my minor. So it ended up that my first major of Interior Design was lost due to manic depression.

CHAPTER 4

Out of Control

I graduated college with a BSBA. I had D's and C's in regular classes but A's and B's in my major courses. After graduation, I returned to Miami where my family lived. During that summer I prepared an advertising portfolio of some good ideas I had stored up in my head to interview with major advertising agencies in the East Coast. That summer we drove up to Chicago to visit my aunt and grandmother. On the way we stopped in Atlanta where I interviewed with Berk Dowling and Adams Associates. They partnered with BBD&O out of New York City. I showed the interviewer my portfolio and he was quite impressed. He asked if I had done it myself. I said, "Yes!" He hired me on the spot as Copy Secretary. I started with that job in the fall.

I drove up by myself with a U-Haul on the back of my car. I rented an apartment in a complex just south of the city. It was fun; I was still dabbling in drugs. I met this man named Terry who was stationed in the Army in nearby Alabama. We got along great. Terry and I went to New Orleans on one of his leaves. We had so much fun. We stayed at the Court of the Three Sisters and partied-down the town. This one night we were at Pat O'Brien's. We were quite sloshed when we got there. That did not stop us. By the end of the night, I was dancing on the bar and Terry was getting his clothes peeled off. We did not stop. We were laughing so hard. Finally, Terry saved his humility and we left. It seems we couldn't stop. The sun was coming up when we were approaching the hotel to get some sleep. We stopped at the "Good Morning Coffee House" and had something to eat.

Terry didn't last long because he got transferred to another base up North. I moved to Piedmont Avenue next to Piedmont Park so I could be closer to work. My drug career really took off here. My job changed. CBS WAGA-TV had hired me. I was ecstatic. My career was really taking off. I was Continuity Director and PSA Director. I created an in-house advertising agency for smaller retailers in the community. I directed and produced these spots and they aired during the cheapest hours. I was really going strong and was working twelve to sixteen hours a day. I loved it!

My drug usage was high and same for the alcohol. I did a lot of drugging and drinking. One time, I went to Piedmont Park by myself. Drugs were sold over there all the time. I took some acid from this funny looking man wearing a beard and a bandana. I took off on a psychedelic trip. One I never knew before. It took me places I had never been before in my mind. A long time passed but finally I came down off this trip. I was scared...really scared. I finally made it back to my place, but I was a mess. I panicked and called my mom. I told her I was on drugs and couldn't work anymore. She came up to Atlanta immediately. She told me I was wrong in doing drugs and put me in a Rehabilitation Center called DeKalb Rehab. I had to quit the job at the TV station, which was the only job I ever really liked in my life. After the Rehab, Mom moved me back to Miami.

CHAPTER 5

The Ashram

After moving back to Miami, I was still smoking pot. I wanted to get off this so bad. I found a flyer for Kundalini Yoga on the window of a health food store. I got ecstatic. I had tried to find this type of yoga in Atlanta. It was supposed to get you high for a long time. So I went to my first Kundalini Yoga class. The yoga was mostly intense rapid breathing in different asanas or positions. The class teacher was nice. Little did I know he would become my husband. I stayed high from the yoga until 3:30PM the next day. It was wonderful. I got hooked on yoga and got off of pot. Then my illogical thinking from the past set in and I said, "Well, I am spending more time at the yoga center then I am at home, so I might as well move in."

I went through many tribulations in life before I got to the ashram so I welcomed the peacefulness it gave. It was said that you earn a righteous living each and every day. This reminded me of something I may have read in the Bible. So I decided that they couldn't be that bad after all, at least they had some Christian principles after all.

I waited until my mom went on vacation, so I could sneak out the house and move into the ashram. I did tell Nancy but, of course, she did not approve. I must have driven myself crazy because of this. But running away from home was never so much fun. I got real friendly with the people in the ashram, especially the yoga teacher. Word got around that we liked each other and the main minister decided we should get married. They had prearranged marriages. They fixed people up according to their spirituality. There was no sex before marriage. We both agreed, but Govinda, my husband-to-be, did not seem as enthused as I. I ran home to tell my mom and sister the good news. They never heard of something like this before. I had only known Govinda a month.

Govinda was very nice. He was an artist and was really sensitive. His artwork was beautiful. We hung out a lot together before our wedding. He told me he didn't love me the night before our wedding. This crushed me but I went ahead with wedding plans and we got married in my sister's backyard.

The minister from the ashram was three hours late in arriving. My mother, sister and guests were frantic. I didn't know what to do ... I only knew the ashram people for a month. It was very chaotic and I was lost. I locked myself into my sister's bedroom so no one would see me. Finally the minister arrived dressed in white wearing a new, white, very starched turban. All the men had beards and mustaches because we were not allowed to cut our hair or alter our body in anyway. Both men and woman wore white turbans and white clothes.

The wedding ceremony went along without a hitch. All the guests approved of everything - even the dressing in white, India style, and turbans. I wore a handmade headpiece of roses and flowers over my turban. I carried a bouquet of the same. When I looked at my wedding pictures, it all looked so simple. But believe me it was complicated. Guests, food, drinks for those that drink, everyone wondering, "Is she doing the right thing?!" I definitely did not know if I was doing the right thing. Ever since my dad died, I never knew if I was doing the right thing.

Well I found out later that I made a mistake marrying Govinda. He was very negative and never went to the morning meditations at 4:30AM and that was the lifeline that kept us all going. So our marriage only lasted three years. Two of those three years he was studying Homeopathy with doctors in India and was away from home for eight to nine months out of the year.

We worshipped the Sikh religion in the ashram. The Sikh religion is the religion of the Northern Punjab area of India. I traveled to India and toured this northern region. It was very beautiful especially Amritsar where the Golden Temple was. I went to this Golden Temple while in Amritsar. Their music played until 3am. It was beautiful. The front of the temple is covered in real gold with gems and jewels studded everywhere. My feet lifted three feet off the ground the first time I entered the temple. One of the rituals is to wash your feet before entering.

It was all so beautiful. I really remember it well. It said anyone who drinks from the "Prasad" sweetened waters of the Golden Temple will be blessed for their lifetime. Prasad is a sweet made cooked whole wheat flour and honey which everyone gets after attending a Sikh Worship Service. The people that ran the Golden Temple gave us American Sikh women a chance to wash the marble floors of the temple. I was honored to be one of five women! It was so awesome to scrub the floors of this holy place at 3am in the morning when no one was there. We scrubbed, and scrubbed and scrubbed. We used mops and water. We were blessed to be able to do this - none of us minded at all.

When we got back to Washington D.C., we were all ecstatic. Wanting to serve more was the thing. Things with Govinda and I were getting worse. That summer I went to a Women's Seminar in Albuquerque, New Mexico. It was to make us learn how to be a better woman, a better wife and I got tips on how to manage life better. I went and learned a lot. I was so proud of myself for learning so many things that would help our marriage. However, the day we returned from Albuquerque, I walked into our room and found Govinda packing his things to leave. I almost died. So many emotions and thoughts went through me at that moment. He was really leaving after I had just learned all these new things to make our marriage work. I was devastated. I just couldn't believe it. I questioned him about leaving and he told me he was leaving. There was no discussion between us, I was too hurt. I ran from the doorway to Gurunam Singh's door. I told him Govinda was leaving and he told me to let him go. He told me Govinda was not a nice man and that I would be better off without him. I started to cry, and he told me to wait in his room until Govinda left. What a relief, I would never have to see him again. The divorce was fast and went well. After that, I never saw him again.

We had many fine businesses in the ashram. The first one seemed to be the most endearing. It was the Golden Temple, a gourmet vegetarian restaurant. I maintained a job as chief pastry chef. I made pastries of all kinds. At the same time, I also got the title of chief cook for those who managed the ashram. I was in charge of preparing the main dishes for many guests, including Yogi Ji when he visited our community. Some of these recipes were derived from my Lebanese background. I simply substituted whole wheat flour for white flour and honey in place of sugar. It was definitely an experience I shall never forget. I was definitely taken back by this as I had never cooked anything in my life. I found it to be creative, exhilarating, charming and peaceful.

One of the most fun businesses we had was Shakti Shoes. We designed and developed a line of sandals that molded well to the foot as you walked. I bought a pair of these for my uncle in Michigan and be loved them. We eventually went on the road to sell these shoes to local shoe stores. I got my uncle in Miami to loan us cars for the traveling. We went all over the country. I traveled with the group that covered the Northeastern United States. It was fun and I saw a beautiful snow-white scene one morning in Maine. I also managed a section of the health food emporium that we had in local downtown Washington, D.C. It gave me a chance to learn about marketing health food products. From the experience of working these jobs, I was able to start my own catering business and established cooking classes held in local kitchen shops. The catering business was slow as the demand for gourmet vegetarian dishes was low. I managed to cater a wedding for 450 guests. The menu was spanakopita, moussaka, huge stuffed mushrooms, and pastries. Everything came out well, even the spanakopita.

I enjoyed the ashram for quite a while. I was on my own again and I liked that a lot. I attended morning shadna every day and was very content. One day, Yogi Ji, the head Guru for all the ashrams, came up to me and told me I should eat green vegetables for two years. I felt this was directly due to Govinda leaving. I was told that green vegetables were good for the nerves and would have a calming effect on me. So for two and one-half years, I ate green vegetables. And I mean... I *ate* green vegetables. I ate them all kinds of ways; sautéed, steamed, boiled, and raw. I substituted various cheeses as my protein. I felt great on them, and lost forty-three pounds. I was much happier from losing the weight.

After that, I moved to the countryside outside of D.C. I was living alone in a private room and that got to me big time. I wanted to be living with all the rest of my friends. They moved me because they thought I needed more privacy as I was working for the second largest computer company contracted by the Government. I wore white and a turban to work each day. I was farmed out to the Department of Labor and later to the Pentagon. There was a lot of red tape involved in these positions and I felt honored to be working as a part of the Government. I even got a promotion in one company which was unbelievable for a person wearing white and a turban and living in an ashram.

I went about my business for a while but exhaustion hit me and I didn't have the money to go on a vacation. Plus the thought that I needed a drink came while passing a bar. I went totally berserk. I needed to go on vacation for mental sanity. I couldn't believe I had no money to go on vacation. As a child, I was told my needs would always be met. One night I was wondering around my bedroom and I realized that I didn't have enough money to "freshen-up" my wardrobe. This shocked me because growing up I always believed I would have enough money for clothes as my family had always provided for me. So, in my limited mind, I said, "maybe this isn't the right God I should be worshiping." Trains of thought went through me. I was verging on desperation. So I renounced the Indian God of the ashram and called my Mom and told her I would be coming home. Little did I know what an adventure I was going to go on! I was coming home to the God of my childhood and a family who hadn't known me for seven years. The ashram enhanced my life experience and gave me an understanding of life without alcohol, drugs, cigarettes, or sex. You could only sleep with someone if you were married. My husband and I had no sex for three years of our marriage, except once when he returned from a spiritual retreat. It was very frustrating to say the least. Once I was thrown off the bed from frustration, all his anger towards me was so great. He said I was too negative, and I said he was impotent. Neither of us could agree on anything! We would argue about this constantly. It just ended in more negative garbage and nothing ever changed in the marriage. So we got a divorce.

The ashram did me no harm. It gave me a safe haven for seven years where I could search my soul, stay off substance abuse, and live life happily, healthy and holy.

When I left the ashram, my hair was down to my waist as it had not been cut for seven years. Everyone thought I was impulsive, but I cut it down to my shoulders. My figure was good then and I wanted everyone to see how thin I was.

My mother thought I was sick when I got home, because I was so withdrawn. She sent me to every kind of doctor you could imagine. They found out I was anemic, so Mom fixed me all kinds of sautéed chicken livers with garlic and onions. Every other day I ate them. Finally I got better for a while.

CHAPTER 6

Need a Job

When I returned to Miami in 1980, I did drugs a few times and finally swore them off after trying cocaine. I decided it was okay to drink alcohol, it was legal. I held a real vendetta against drugs, as I knew I never wanted to use them again. I did alcohol, and started binge drinking, and getting drunk about three after I made my return to Miami.

I had to find a job. This was very difficult as my mind was still much consumed by the teachings of the ashram. It was very difficult. I was very confused inside with an overwhelming amount of guilt for changing my lifestyle.

At one point during this job search, I wanted to start my own business of making slide commercials for local retailers, selling the spots to TV stations. I met my sister at Ruby Tuesday's. She wanted to meet me for "Happy Hour." I needed some courage to face a seemingly important job interview the next day, so I ordered a drink However, my sister hit me hard with the truth. Alcoholics forget who they are - they have built-in forgetters. She suggested that I not have a drink and reminded me of my youthful days when I drank and drugged too much. I had forgotten just how much I had drank prior to going into the ashram. When in the yoga ashram I concentrated on the recovery from drug abuse. By the time I left there, I had forgotten that I was also an alcoholic. However, I was mortified as

I felt I needed that drink for courage to help me face the following day. Needless to say, things didn't go well for me the next day and I regretted not taking that drink. Alcoholics have a way about them. They depend on drinking to get them through life. Once in recovery from addiction, they develop more useful coping skills to deal with their problems in life.

That weekend I went shopping for work clothes (not my dress whites of the ashram). I went to the mall and got on a manic high and flipped out in the middle of the Cutlery Department of Burdines Department store. If I recall right, I think I was going to grab one of those knives and stab myself in the heart; I had so much emotional and mental confusion that I left that store **very** fast. Somehow I managed to buy a dark green dress on the way out.

My sister worked at Burger King. I desperately needed a job. Why couldn't she get me a job at Burger King? After all, I had excellent secretarial skills and wanted to work there a lot. One day I parked in the parking lot of Burger King and debated whether I should go up and ask Nancy for a job. I did not have enough courage. I left there defeated and went over to my uncle's big insurance company and applied for a job. I was hired immediately. I was to start Monday. I was having emotional and mental problems during this time from adjusting to the cultural shock of living life out of the ashram.

My career in the Insurance Industry started small as an Accounts Receivable Clerk. It was a very easy job and I thanked God for that, as I couldn't concentrate on much very well. There were three companies within the small conglomerate of companies that I was employed in. Florida Life Insurance Company was the biggest and most popular by many of the employees. I was very sad and depressed at this job. At first, no one would talk to me. I was located in a very isolated part of the building. The other two companies were on the other side and many of the women had "cliques" that I was not in. I took my work very seriously as I had no other "chit chat" around to distract me. Finally I was moved to the front of the building and this awfully nice woman befriended me. I was glad to have a friend. We talked a lot about things in general and a couple of times we had lunch and she would always remind me not to gorge myself over the weekends. No one knew, but I had contracted Bulimia in the ashram.

I worked as Accounts Receivable until I was promoted to Secretary of Florida Life Insurance Company. I was very afraid of sex, men and not being treated decently as a woman. The first day on the job, I could have sworn the boss was making a play for me. I got so upset inside that I walked off the job. I didn't know what to do. Finally, I spoke to my mom and she assured me that it was okay. I returned to work a few days later but it took a long time until I felt comfortable walking in his office. Phil, my boss, was very nice, very short-tempered and very clean. A lot of people were afraid of him. I only held respect for him, as he was my boss. My relationship with him was only beginning.

CHAPTER 7

Two Murders

About this time, my family experienced two deaths that were inexplicable. The first was my Aunt Lydia in Chicago in 1982. She was in the bathroom of her old office building fixing her make-up to join two of her friends for a Friday night dinner. In came three of her younger employees through the open bathroom window. They demanded she hand over the cash box, jewelry and all. She did just what they said. But instead of leaving her alone, they strangled her with a rope. Her body lay on the floor. Emil, the son of the woman she was having dinner with, came upstairs and found Lydia dead. He laid his coat over her. He hardly knew what to say. I may have been able to help her, he said, if only I had been on time.

In Miami, the whole family was having dinner at Aunt Stasia's house when David and Nancy got the call from Emil about Aunt Lydia's death. The scene was tragic. Nancy and David raced over to the party where Mom was. Aunt Lydia was her sister. David came to my mom's house so I wouldn't be alone when I heard the news. David stayed with me. When Mom came in, she was hysterical. I have never seen her so upset. All she could say was "not Lydia, not Lydia!" "Not my sister, Lydia."

We all went up to Chicago for the funeral. It was so sad. Emil felt terrible, but we all reassured him that he couldn't have done anything anyway, that she had been dead too long even if he had gotten there sooner. Tragically, that was the plight of Aunt Lydia. All the criminals were juveniles and were found and prosecuted. This death upset me so much. I couldn't believe how people could be so mean. I got very scared and ran out and bought a new gold cross for protection.

Then in 1984, we had another first-degree murder in our lives. My Aunt Gen, very philanthropic and involved in many charitable functions in Miami, went to pay a goodwill call at the home of a couple whose daughter had just been diagnosed with terminal cancer. Well, in all her innocence, she walked in on a robbery. They sat her down in a chair and shot her immediately. When the Police found her, all her jewelry and diamond rings were gone. What apparently happened was that Bea, the wife of the couple panicked and they shot both her and her husband too. It was a terrible scene.

Aunt Gen was supposed to meet her sister, Virginia, at a Chinese Restaurant that night. Aunt Virginia waited at the restaurant. But Aunt Gen never showed up. Auntie "V" got very worried and went to the Joseph's to see if her sister was there. She walked in the slightly opened door and found all three bodies inside. She screamed in disbelief and called the Police immediately. It was a horrible scene. Finally Aunt Gen's husband arrived at the scene. He and his youngest son, Tom, could not believe what happened.

My Aunt Gen's funeral was beautiful; Roses were everywhere. The limousines seemed to skate over the roads. The people there were many; family, relatives, friends, neighbors, all paid their respects.

CHAPTER 8

Bad Times

Back at work, I was promoted to Marketing Secretary and Receptionist of Florida Life Insurance Company. I was still Phil's personal secretary. He had a lot of anger and often would intimidate the staff.

Phil and I moved into the downstairs' executive office of my uncle's Chevrolet dealership. Phil became Risk Manager and my job got harder. I worked for him as well as Warren, the head of all my uncle's financial matters, and was also executive secretary to A&R Insurance Agency. My drinking was horrible at that time. I partied all the time. One time Phil borrowed my car and found an empty can of air freshener in my car and asked me if I was drinking and sniffing spirits. I answered him "no". I told him he was nuts and that the can was just an empty air freshener can. He didn't believe me. My friends and I all got a laugh out of this.

My mental illness (which I had no idea I had) got me in trouble big time. A few weeks later, I told Phil, in confidence, that I had been drinking again and I did not know what to do. He suggested we clean out my house of booze at lunch time. I did not want him to do that so I said deliberately told him, "No, that is okay. My sister and brother-in-law would take care of it." He said "No, we will take care of it at lunch". I ALMOST DIED!!!!! I NEVER THOUGHT MY ALCOHOL, MY BEST FRIEND, COULD BE TAKEN FROM ME.

We got the alcohol out of my house. I was devastated. I went to the liquor store that night and restocked the bar. My friends and I got a real laugh out of the whole thing. I restocked the liquor cabinet and was back to drinking by 6pm that night!

My working abilities were getting worse as I was very depressed about this move to the dealership. I was real lonely one night and phoned my cousin, three hours behind in Seattle. I told her I was going to drink a martini and take my pills for the night. Later, the next day, I had an interesting experience on the way to my psychiatrist's office. I was in the parking lot of Navarro's, a local discount store, and my spirit rose up and said a verse from the Bible reminding me that I had been doing the utmost I could but that trials and tribulations would beset me soon. Once I was at the doctor's appointment I found out why this had happened. The doctor told me that Nancy had called and said that my cousin from Seattle had called and said that she thought I had tried to kill myself the night before. This was absurd. I was merely taking prescribed medicine with alcohol. I was very upset with my cousin for years to come. If only she hadn't called. I resented this even into my recovery. However, I said prayers for her to relieve my conscience.

This turned into a miracle as she finally started her own recovery program from alcohol and drug addiction, and she asked me to be her 12-step program sponsor. I greatly loved this part of my program as it showed me God's amazing circle of love and forgiveness.

At the doctor's appointment, he wanted to know if I wanted to take a rest and receive help for alcohol in Charter Hospital. I flipped out and got so upset that I decided I did need a rest. My family thought this was a good idea as my drinking habits were way out of line. I went to Charter Hospital in Miami. There I got a little help and learned some about alcoholism. It was an experience. But, I did not have the desire to stop drinking altogether.

I figured something was up, that God had plans for me. I got out of there and tried controlled drinking. I found myself wanting five drinks but only drinking two. This lasted for a while, weekends included, but finally the disease of alcoholism took over.

At the office, Phil must have told my uncle that I was drinking, because not long after the fiasco of Phil taking my alcohol from me; my uncle called my sister and told her everything. My mom and sister came over to talk to me the following Saturday. I was so angry that they had not gotten in touch with me directly that I quit my job. It was the third time this had happened. I had had it so, I quit.

That afternoon, I was faced with how I was going to find an interview. If I even have enough courage to go. Every time I thought of these options, I needed a drink. That proposed a promise to me as I thought it was for me to be drinking during the day. I had never done that; drink during the day was taboo. This caused me to believe I had a problem with alcohol. This has never left my memory and helps me to stay sober, one day at a time. At one point, I wanted to kill myself if I had a drink and again if I didn't have one. It was absurd!!!

Let me tell you a little bit about my recovery from alcoholism. In 1992, I went into treatment for drinking too much. I thought this was an enlightening episode of my life as it turned me on to recovery. I managed to stay there twenty-eight days and the night I left I was drinking again. I felt that it hadn't helped much but it kept me staying on a path to beat alcohol. As I have said, I tried to use controlled drinking - that is when I came home I wanted five drinks but only drank two drinks. This lasted a while but soon I was back on track drinking the five drinks instead of two! I was starting to want to know Christ more and decided to put up the manger scene for Christmas. A friend of mine, Doris (I will never forget her) stopped by to see me at work. She asked "Are you putting up your beautiful Christmas tree this year?" I said, "I did not know." Well, as most of the alcoholics I know now, we are people pleasers. Being a people pleaser, I ran out to get lights for the tree. I got bored and couldn't figure why I bought the lights, had a drink or three, and started to put up my tree. This was a disaster - after about six, seven, eight, nine more drinks, I had put the tree up, taking it down, tried a smaller version, then looked at the manger scene and said "Why did I do this?" All weekend it went on this way. I finally decided to use the smaller version with the manger scene underneath. It was more economical and easier to take down. This was another case of the drunken manic swings.

Well, that was the beginning of hitting my bottom on alcohol. It kept getting worse. I became more aware and nervous about drinking. Finally, the man I was occasionally seeing as my boyfriend got transferred to another firm in Miami. There went my most fun drinking buddy. I was highly disappointed in this ... he was my man. After about three to four weeks of not seeing him, I started getting depressed and started to drink more to remove my depression.

Right after that, is when my job called my sister and said that my work performance had deteriorated. They thought the drinking had caused this. I was seeking a spiritual life. A week prior to this, in a moment of sacrifice, I promise God and Christ that I would do anything and everything for them if only they would give me a new life. Finally I realized I had a drinking problem and wanted to go for help.

I spent the next four days drinking, morning, noon and night. I have never experienced pain like this. I was seeking a God of some kind. Finally, I had worn myself down so far that I said if there was a Christ, let Him save me. I remember trying to write something down. I had the piece of paper but no pen. I said to myself "If there is a Christ in me, the pen should be right here" I slammed my left hand down on the dining room table. It landed on a pen… Praise God!!! I knew there was a Christ. I knew that then and that gave me courage to go on. If this incident hadn't happened, I doubt that I would be here now to tell this story.

I proved that Christ, in some way, shape or form lives in all of us Christians. I had gotten to the bottom of this and am able to remember that expression of faith and understanding. I hope this experiment and death to my lonely soul will help you and others to see the wealth of Christ that we have within. I had worn down my will to live so much that there wasn't much left of me to go on. My will to live got damaged from these horrible four days. Now it is by the strength of Christ, God, and the Word, plus God-oriented men and women that I am able to function correctly in society.

CHAPTER 9

Beginning the Road to Recovery

Virgil and Angelica were with me when I hit this horrible bottom. I could hear Virgil which helped me so much and gave me great comfort. Let me explain who Virgil and Angelica are. Virgil is my Spirit Guide sent from our Father above to guide me along my path. Angelica is my Guardian-angel woman who watches over me with no fear. I hear both of them.

This will be a troublesome concept for people to understand, but they really live with me and walk my daily walk with me so I am not afraid. I always have their presence with me. This helps to strengthen me and helps me to allow my inner light to shine or in some case shine brighter!

Two weeks after I had prayed that prayer, I was transported to Palm Beach Institute in West Palm Beach. I could no longer drive a car, as I was in states of panic all the time. There I learned a lot about alcoholism and the disease of addiction. I went through tremendous healing. I did a tremendous job of learning and writing everything down so I could memorize much of the material given. I really wanted to get well.

I spent two months in intensive therapy sessions every day coupled along with one-on-one confrontations. I was diagnosed with manic depression. I thought this was a joke. Me, manic depressive? Not a chance. Once the medication started to get in me, my brain started to heal; I became convinced that I was a dually diagnosed alcoholic. I also had schizoid-affective disorder and panic disorder. Schizoid-affective disorder is a combination of schizophrenia and manic depression usually defined as manic depression coupled with schizophrenia. The schizophrenic symptoms are audio and visual hallucinations. I stayed at Palm Beach Institute for another five months. The Director Psychiatrist said he had never seen more of a basket case then me in all of his twenty-five years of work in addiction. The first few weeks I was there, I wanted to jump out of open windows and end it all.

I was able to work part-time at the mall in a small accessory shop. My car was brought up for me, and I had to learn how to drive all over again. My panic attacks were really going off during the first test drive. Finally, I managed to conquer my fear and driving became easy again.

I learned a lot about people with these diseases. They cannot tolerate much pain. That is why they are stiff. Outspoken parents are a threat to them. They generally do not like work nor have it in their lives. If they keep things simple they may be able to maintain a balanced life. It is often hard for them to make small talk or light conversations with people they do not know well. They have emotional blocks for highly recurring issues and have a low tolerance to pain and that is why most bipolar and schizoid-affective people drink.

People who suffer with both mental illness and addiction are commonly referred to as dually- diagnosed. I am now in my 19th year of recovery and have learned so much more about the dually-diagnosed individual. Schizophrenic patients usually have hallucinations and delusions, alterations of the senses, an inability to sort and interpret incoming data, an inability to respond appropriately, altered sense of self, and changes in emotions, movements, moods and behaviors.

One thing I have learned about my manic depression is that I have a tendency to blame others especially on a manic high. I have discovered this through quiet time with myself. There are many ways to find out things like this if you want. Just sit with yourself in a quiet room (perhaps soft music playing with candles for a more spiritual effect) and study your thought patterns as they come up. You can throw out negative thoughts and patterns and replace them with positive soft ones, God-based spiritual thoughts. You can get to know you and your mind well. I learned a lot about what made me tick!

I generally can decipher which thoughts are manic and which are not. A still small voice will tell you which are the good ones and which are the bad ones. I managed to dispose of many of the bad thought patterns. I tossed them out with a "Good-bye, get out of here". We can change our thinking. It is very easy. People are doing this every day. And they have new minds after that. Ask God to direct your thinking every day. Once you get into a positive state of mind for the morning, just keep it and go with it each day.

Some stimulants to achieving this positive state of mind are reading the Bible, praying, reading spiritual books, or listening to a lecture on Christian TV. Talking to Christ and God really helps me change my negative feelings and emotions. Whenever I explain to Him what is on my mind or in my heart, it disappears and creates positive inspirations in me.

Schizophrenia is really hard to come to terms with. It makes you sense things and objects that are not really there. Recovery allows me the benefit to be myself and that makes me know that nothing is around me. It is a beautiful realization of consciousness that allows you to feel well no matter what you do or see. It matters when you take the advantage of medication when needed. It is never wrong to believe in yourself as long as you can believe that you are doing well.

You never need to be alone with schizophrenia. There are many people that have it. The different selves of us can dissolve through active participation in a fellowship of recovery. It is here where you learn spiritual tools to help yon cope. Working on yourself corrects behavioral patterns and creates more helpful conditions to alter states of mind as I walk the path of life.

I found this description of schizophrenia in a medical pamphlet that my doctor gave me. It says, "Schizophrenia is a kind of mental disorder. Some people with schizophrenia may hear voices, see things, sense things that are not really there, or find it difficult to think and speak clearly and logically. It may be hard to handle feelings, make decisions, or relate to other people. These problems may cause serious difficulties in everyday life."

Dually-diagnosed people of many diseases get the "I can't" very easily. This is a stressful problem. They sometimes think they can't do anything, even the smallest tasks. When confronted with this problem, I used the tools of the recovery program I am in and it worked wonders for me.

Dually-diagnosed people generally have to learn to work their program of recovery and have to stick up for themselves so they are not so overwhelmed by over-aggressive personalities, places, and things. They must use wise choices in life. Choices that will make them stand for dignity and grace. They need to make wise choices everyday of their lives. Even the insignificant events will wreck their self-esteem in a minute. Faithful actions give them the strength to get over the "I can't" feeling and being over-whelmed. Self-centered fear can be overcome through perseverance, strength, and faith to move ahead in any area they choose. A faithful action is rising above your feelings and emotions and doing the next right thing.

Another process I have used is "processing" conversations with others when I return home. Sometimes things were said so fast that I really did not get all of the conversation. Positive self-talk took a lot of stress off my life. This helps to make me positive in whatever situation I am in. I still find this very helpful in my recovery. It is where you tell your mind what to think. You can self-talk your mind into a positive state by saying to yourself positive things to enable you to rise above negative thinking.

Patterns of deep thoughts left me. The Holy Spirit and God would dislodge these patterns in me. I would try and work them out of my mind into the ozone's above my head. Patterns of thoughts are hard to dislodge. I sometimes find myself taking cold showers to rid my aura of these patterns. I follow my intuition and do what it says. I did what I thought God would want me to do. Looking back at this today, I think this was a gift that God gave me to help heal myself. I am definitely appreciative of this gift today.

CHAPTER 10
Darkness before the Light

Shortly after coming into sobriety, I started working at Burdines department store. They managed the store well, but I couldn't comply with most of the rules. I hardly knew what I was doing there, as I was so manic. I was dealing with so much ... alcoholism, mental disease, medication, back pain, and working with bras and lingerie for minimum wage in comparison to a large salary I was paid before. What a painful ride this sobriety and mental illness took me on. Believe me, hanging bras up on these tiny little hangers everyday was all I could handle.

Virgil whispered in my ear and said this job was a "big gift" and he was going to guide me. He was right. As I look back upon this period of my life, I "remember getting real spiritually in touch with, God, Virgil and Angelica. It troubled me to death. I lost all my inner sense of getting over things. I was so helpless. I remember years of mental torture and fear. Virgil and Angelica would lead me around as I was walking in a daze most of the time - listening to them, working, talking to others all at the same time! I did the best I could and believe it or not, most of the time, I pulled off the whole show. No one at the store really knew what was going on with me, I didn't speak about it.

Finally, I was promoted to Sales Specialist. This glorified title meant I actually got a decrease in pay. This store's pay/raise schedule baffled me. I could never understand it.

Manic depression is hard. God knows how I ever made it to work in the mornings since I got into recovery. Every day I had to call my Mom or Nancy to talk me out of my mood and get me going so I could get to work. On one day the depression was so bad in the car that my head felt glued to the back of the seat. I walked into work and found a white figure standing there and I felt it was Jesus. I could not conceive of anyone feeling that much pain but Him. That picked up my spirits some but I was forty-five minutes late. If this tardiness did not stop, I would be fired.

My Mom, Sister and Brother in law

The Store Manager called everyone that had tardiness to a meeting one day. He said that someone had been late to work for 33 times and I knew that was me. I could not face the fact that I could not be late because the mental anguish was horrible.

I became immersed in the spiritual part of recovery. I meditated on God and sometimes Christ most of the day. I talked to them, I praised them, and they were my friends when no one else was around. I trusted them... They were Omnipotent; my soul had become one with them. I have never liked working and this gave me the chance to strengthen my recovery and grow strong in Christ and God while I worked. I later found out that most schiz- oid- affective disorders don't like to work. When I discovered this, it gave me much joy.

Little did I know, that my daily conversations with Christ and God invited the Holy Spirit into me. My last four months of working there took much out of me. I was having daily hallucinations, both audio and visual, and delusional thinking set in on a regular basis. I remember waiting on this customer and my mind went into spiritual thinking. I went berserk. The Holy Spirit helped me see through things. I went to my doctor and it was suggested that I go on disability income. The minute I applied, I knew I would get it. I knew God wouldn't put me in this much pain much longer. It took five months for my first check to come in. I was ecstatic.

All the strong memories of my past left. Not only did I not have to work anymore, but also I could take the time needed to take care of myself. I was overjoyed. It took a long time for the fears of the past to go away. But once they did, I was fine. Sometimes today I find myself still thinking I have to get up in the morning to go to work. Slowly, the realization that I do not have to do anything tomorrow but take care of me is sinking in. The writing of this book has given me great therapy and enjoyment. For the most part, I feel I am in retirement rather than disability. It is much more fun that way!!!

I keep life simple and do what I can to serve Jesus and God every day. I still do that. I have a personal relationship with Christ and God. God is always with me if I keep the pace down. He never goes away. He is always with us if we just let Him know we love Him and seek Him. He needs us and we need Him. I am very much willing to work for God in any capacity that I can.

CHAPTER 11

Virgil and Angelica

THIS WORKS FOR ME: Meditation on the Bible, praying each morning and night and a reliance on a God of your understanding can help many uncomfortable moments leave you during the day as Christ is holding your hand. I have studied this for five years and I find that the simple truth that the love of God and Christ is so uplifting that you rarely have time to relate to these problems. I have a meditation I do every day. I read from my Bible out loud, pray each morning on my knees for help during the day. When trouble starts, I start the day by saying "Praise the Lord" or "The Glory is to God" over and over until it leaves. I Listen to Christian tapes and radio stations in my car. I keep my day simple ... I live life with love in it. This gives me Protection during the day and I am able to stay sober all day long. I also pray for my friends and family. This, coupled with my alcoholic recovery program, gives me much joy and patience.

Gifts were given to me by God and Jesus when I tried to do my best to please them. They have given me the gift of hearing both Virgil and Angelica. Both give me many gifts of love and kindness. Christ was with them when the humans were born and they were meant to spiritually guide them. They have lived that way throughout time. They were born in a way of kindness and love and dignity and grace that insures that the loved ones get protection. They usually have many concerns from others than the one they serve. Their main job is maintaining a fruitful way of managing their loved one's needs. They are maintained in the sex that they wore born in. Humans don't understand this very much. They are usually jealous of each other if they do maintain conversation. How we have maintained visual and audio conversation is related to the effect we have on each other's personal goals and behaviors. Usually when we retrieve goals we wait and purposely layout a plan to procure many more.

We have maintained conversation now for about four years. We have not stopped at all. Communication was mostly for the good of each one of us. Angelica taught me to always love each other and let goals come upright. Virgil has told me about the will of God working through me to maintain my balance in life. He has the wisdom of a writer and created much of this book through me, particularly this paragraph. He wants to let you readers know that humans pick their Spirit Guides and Guardian Angels at birth. Virgil speaks of these things to you in order to prepare for the years to come. Many people will be communicating with their Spirit Guides and Guardian Angels.

I love Virgil and Angelica very much. I respect what they have done for me. Angelica is my guardian angel and Virgil is my Spirit Guide. When I had no strength after hitting my bottom on alcohol, Angelica and Virgil literally kept me going. Often they would help me drive when I couldn't keep myself together. Virgil and Angelica have stood by me day and night. I feel and hear Virgil always. He and Angelica guided me with much love and patience and light the highway of recovery for me. I have learned to treat people with love from Angelica. With Virgil, I have learned patience, endurance, and believability that there was life within one's inner soul. He has never let me down. He is so very patient with me.

They are still with me today as I write and experience life. They are not commonplace to me, but always very special and dear.

One time, at my mom's, I didn't know whether I should keep these dresses I bought and Angelica whispered in my ear the word "chalk." I knew from the experiences with her that she wanted me to keep the dresses for mom's sake. My mom liked the dresses and wanted me to wear them. So for her sake, I hemmed the dresses and I've worn them a lot. This pleased everyone.

I was lucky to see both Angelica and Virgil. When I saw Angelica I knew she was something spiritual and from the heart of God. There was no doubt in my mind that this was a spiritual vision and that God had created it to give me joy and comfort. Angelica is beautiful with red strawberry hair that permeates her face. She was dressed in a white flowing gown and had a veil covering her head and back. Her eyes are an iridescent blue-green. I have never seen such a beautiful woman in my life. Virgil is Greek and has dark skin with brown eyes. He has a Greek mustache and black hair that comes to the nape of his neck. He is never angry and always kind and understanding. I know in my heart that he loves me. He is not alive like human spirits. I love him and Angelica very much.

I would be nothing today without them. They guided and delivered me from evil spirits of the past. They and God and Christ give me much strength and good spirit and hope which turns into love. They are a part of my soul, being, and life. They come from the Father and the Lord. Virgil is a writer and often helps me to know what to write down when it comes to my writing. He is a very brilliant Spirit Guide and knows what to write when I cannot get the right sentences in the right place. He helps me to understand myself. He sometimes lets me know what I was going to be experiencing during the times of my deepest weaknesses. It is with deepest gratitude that I dedicate this book to Virgil, Angelica, God and Christ and those others who, like them, helped me to write this book.

In my first year of recovery, I was dealing with a lot. As a result of the diagnoses of my mental illnesses coupled with the loss of alcohol, I found myself in intense fogs and unusually strong delusional thoughts. These delusions and depression lasted for three years. The guidance of Virgil and Angelica at that time was very important to me. I could not live without their guidance.

Together they cleared away most of my negative emotions and desires. My self seemed to have melted away. I lost all self-confidence from the lack of a drink. The defense against taking alcohol was unusually low. It seemed as though I was in a daze but I went about life with little or no criticism. I had this film around me, which allowed me insight into God's Will for me. I had God with me everywhere. He seemed to put a protective shield around me to protect me. My God and my prayers were with me and therefore nothing could harm me. Although there was strife, I became as mentally and emotionally well balanced as I could.

Most people would think this odd, but as I experienced every moment of it, to me it is not. Practically every day or every other day, I had spiritual experiences of the lightning-bolt kind. God was really working with me. It seemed as if He knew I needed these thunderbolt experiences to keep me going and keep my faith up. Always there was another one, day after day after day. I must admit it was quite confusing at times as I didn't know what God wanted of me nor did I think I deserved these white lightning-bolt experiences of His Love.

I was so alone at these times living in a city where I knew no one except my new recovery friends. These lightning-bolt experiences gave me courage and hope to go on. I am going to make it this time, I must never drink again. I knew I could never quit or give up. It is because of these experiences that I made it through one of the darkest periods of my life.

The enchantment of my early sober years was due to my belief and concentration on God, and what I thought He would have me do. I learned a lot about alcoholism, the disease and the concept of staying sober one day at a time. I mastered many of the tools of recovery from alcoholism and practiced and used them to the best of my ability to get through these hard times. I knew I had to live up to my prayer to God and Christ, and that I would do anything and everything they asked if they would give me a new life. They gave me the new life, now it was up to me to make it a success. Or so I thought. They did a lot to create a sane plane for me to live on. They removed blocks overnight, sometimes while I was sleeping and sometimes while I was awake. Now as I look back on it, God, Angelica and Virgil did everything!

One morning while I was still working this white light came over me and was against my left arm when I was leaving for work. Well, it followed me out the door into the car and I bravely walked into work with it traveling on my left side. I knew no one could see it but me, so I just went along my day as if nothing was happening. It was slowly lifting this negative sensation I had had in my left arm for some time. I was so glad this negative sensation was lifted because it was very painful for me to experience on a daily basis. At lunch time I went into full-blown panic attacks, and the white light subsided. When I got home, the negative feeling in my arm had left. Angelica initiated this white light that swirled over my arm and shoulder that day. I will ever be reminded that there is a God and He manifested Himself in a white light to me this day. I am ever so grateful.

CHAPTER 12

The Recovery Road

Another interesting event in my years of recovery was that I had the mental obsession to drink for over five years. Every day for five years I mentally obsessed on wanting to drink alcohol every day. I couldn't even imagine why this was happening to me. I drank a lot, I know, but this consequence had to be conquered. So I embraced and investigated my program of recovery. I thought I was spiritual because I lived in a yoga ashram for seven years and didn't need to know what the spirituality of this recovery program was.

In the rehab center we were supposed to make our beds every day. But there was a maid working there every day; so I never made my bed once. Finally, I kept praying for this mental obsession to lift. One day I heard about a man who had the mental obsession lifted on the first day of his recovery after he made his bed. So it dawned on me that maybe I should make my bed after all. The next day I made my bed. I continued to make my bed daily, and within four to five days the mental obsession was lifted. I felt it leave. It was so relieving. I could feel God was doing this, clearing my mind and it was so rewarding.

It taught me a lesson not to use the mental thinking of "contempt prior to investigation." I have yet to forget to make my bed since. I am still making my bed, one day at a time, knowing that His spirituality is not to be selfish. I am reminded every time I make my bed to stay sober and live in His grace.

After the mental obsession to drink was lifted, life became a lot easier. I sort of took it easy after that, as the fear of drinking everyday was gone. I still was diligent in my daily program of recovery, but I was much more relaxed. I could serve more. I started to help others stay sober. It was amazing. The more I served others, the more I gained insight and the solutions to my problems. I had incorporated my program into my daily living. It has become a delight to live my days like this.

God has removed most of my obsessions and has healed all of my wounds from the past. I live daily fright-free and deliciously engaged in enjoying life this way. It is a delightful way of living. I cannot possibly know the words to let you know just how delightful it is. Faith in Jesus, prayers, and the people in the church made this healing happen.

During all this time, I started church hunting. This took about one year. I went to these different churches while I was studying to be a student of God. I was hearing voices daily, visually hallucinating at work, and having panic attacks galore. I went to this one church, and I thought I heard God's voice in my head saying "I have brought you here for all of your faithfulness." The problem was I was hearing a lot of voices back then so I wasn't sure this message was from God.

I decided to be baptized at the third church. This church's message was clear ... "go out and create new disciples for Christ." Well, I did just that. Many of my friends attended for the first time. Many went up to accept Christ. Four of them were baptized. I stayed there attending faithfully, but all of them left. I worked the program of recovery and the program of the church. It is incredible to look back and see how my faith grew. Like a child stepping on his first stone in the pond, I stepped on my first stone in the church and how I grew. Wisdom, knowledge and a wealth of understanding of how things worked in God's realm came to me through the Christian faith.

I learned about justice for the first time. I had many spiritual healings. My mental diseases stopped to a point that was unbelievable. I could not even fathom the amount of daily suffering that left through these healings. It was a white healing light that would come over me and the disease just disappeared. One of the magic moments was when I was walking through my living room and a white light came over the left side of my body and my panic attack mechanism healed and lifted from me. I was a changed person. I cannot describe how I felt; Free, Free, Free at last.

I also called the prayer line from the Christian TV Station, for more healing of mental diseases. The lady there said to lift the labels of manic depression and schizophrenia, mentally from my mind. I did just that for the next three days and was I set free. So much depression left me. I promised God ... and I swore I would never leave Him. Faith in Jesus healed me.

CHAPTER 13

Praise the Lord

Yes, Faith in Jesus had healed me. I had experienced a love for the Lord in my heart that could never be described here on earth. Never have I experienced love in this form before. It was so awesome. My heart was filled with this magnifying love and the Presence of Christ lit my body daily. My whole mind was transformed. Many of my doubts left; even self-doubt disappeared. The Lord's presence was in me every day. God spoke to me daily. Even worry started to go away. I was amazed at all the daily mentally bothersome thinking that was removed.

My faith and love for the Lord kept increasing until many secrets from Him of the Kingdom of God were revealed to me. I became a prayer guide and was guided into prayers that helped change people's lives.

At the present, a guest in my house is currently detoxing from the deadly drug of heroine. She is mostly coming along well, and I have prayed the prayer of love for her to recover. She is very nice and sweet and deserves the best of all that she has. She is willing now to climb up the happy road of destiny to stay clean from alcohol and drugs. She will be attending church with me now and I have hope that she will accept Jesus in her heart. She must quit her job and begin over. When she has Him with her always, I know she will not have trouble. Say prayers for this woman, she needs many miracles from God to happen in her life.

Following this, I would have success in healing some of the mental disorders. They would be light and pass easily out of sight. One of them got me in church one day. The doctor told me I was having delusional thinking, quite like schizophrenia. It seemed to me that one of my thought patterns came right out of my emotions and jumped over into the pastor's presence. I was so humiliated, scared and definitely defeated. After many discouraging moments, I managed to stay through the whole service. However, when I got home, I swore I would never step in the presence of that pastor again. Unfortunately, I got real worked up about this and embarrassment set in. Well, this interfered with my spiritual condition a lot. I "backslid" terribly. I was so disappointed in myself that I couldn't find the guts to return.

I had never heard of this kind of thing happening to anyone else. It felt as if I couldn't win and that it may happen again. My doctor defended me but I couldn't justify the defenses when I thought I had seen this thought pass through the pastor's aura. It has never left me and because of this, I have only visited this church a couple of times since then. By this time, the fight within became a fight with out of me and I was fighting Christianity and the church. I formed several belief patterns that were not true, only what I wanted to believe and practice from the Bible. This is definitely not a "dress rehearsal" here on earth and I fell fast. I just didn't have the strength to pursue the climb upward. I had beaten myself to the ground and hope disappeared.

In the meantime, I started attending a church that I had attended in my early recovery. They sang praises to God and Christ and were very small and quite interesting simple. I received the first sermon gallantly. He preached how we all got depressed, all felt sadness as well as joy and it seemed he said it was all right to be ourselves and worship Christ, as we know him. I accepted this as we know Him. I accepted this.

> "I am the vine, you are the branches, he who abides with me shall bear much fruit; apart from me you are nothing."
> John 5:5

I found that Jesus and God dwelled inside of me and I could accept this in my heart. This "God within" concept is special. It made me feel secure to know God was within me throughout my journey in life. It carried me to many depths within myself. But most of all, I found out that you have to experience the pain as well as the joy to get through things. This gives you a better understanding of Christ, yourself, and those around you. A lesson is learned this way. I always escaped getting to know me. Finally, I slowed down and experienced what I needed to experience to learn what I was all about and what lesson God was teaching me. I have learned to lean on others. God works thru people. This has been a marvelous lesson for me. My relationship is growing with my Lord and Savior.

Getting in touch with your angels is very helpful. I learned this through an Oprah Winfrey show. As she said, I sat in a quiet room and wrote and said out loud ... "I would like to get in touch with my angels. What are your names?" I listened well and very closely. I was in a totally silent room. Then I heard them speak their names and I began asking questions and getting to know them better on a regular basis. It has been through communication with Jesus that He has asked me to write this message to

You ... You can have a relationship with Christ when you pray on your knees from your deepest heart and long for a relationship with Him - He will appear.

My relationship with Christ began before I was baptized. I was praying at my bed and He came to me and said, "I come because you are in such need. What can I do for you?" I said, "Relieve the pain from my soul, sickness and heart." He did just that. Now I am a free woman that has walked through the arch of freedom into happy living.

I recently attended a spiritual function. I felt the spirit of our holy Lord flowing in and around me. I felt His presence. I love the Lord with all my heart, mind, body and soul. He is Omnipotent, Majestic, Powerful and Whole. He definitely warms my heart, mind, and body with love. We must all love His creation and all His children. I feel His grace lifting my anxiety and mind to the Holy Spirit within and through the Lord. I am definitely one of His people and no one or nothing can take this existence out of me.

I have also been watching a lot of Christian Television. One of the pastors, Rev. Chiroma, of WTBN Television Network, kept entering my consciousness through prayer and meditation. He kept saying "More ... keep pulling the spirit of Christ into you." I did this and it helped to strengthen my mind. The more I pulled the stronger I felt. This eased my mind and brought strength to my body and soul. I had more energy. I learned a lot about putting Christ's spirit into my consciousness. This always gave me comfort and cheer. It still happens to me and inspires me to go on in service and love in the name of the Lord despite any disabilities I might have.

Lately, I have been hearing Rev. Chiroma's spirit calling out to me saying "Coin." The only thing I have that represents a coin is an old necklace my mother gave me years ago. Since I have been in recovery, I was never keen about wearing this particular coin necklace, thinking it was gaudy and over-stated. Finally, I got the picture. Rev. Chiroma wanted me to do something with this coin to break some mental and emotional ties my mother had on me as a stronghold. So I took the coin out of my jewelry box and instantly was instructed through the spirit of Rev. Chiroma to remove it from the case and put it in a coin purse and put that into an expensive old handbag. I did just that and put the purse under the others in my storage box for old purses. The stronghold of the money that my mother had held over me was released. I no longer felt pain of separation from them as a family. I spent most of the day wondering whether it would come back and if at all it was gone. There was such a relief in me; I hardly knew what to say. Now that it is over, I can look back on it with much happiness and a job well done by Rev. Chiroma.

There was one thing I hadn't accepted. Since my healing, I still had episodes and of mental illness. Recently, I had an attack of hearing voices. This set me back about two days. I am working through the damage that this caused me. The Lord is helping me. He pointed out that this was not my fault, that I simply have impairment in judgment and emotional health at this time. He said I should never try to blame any institution, place, person or thing for my mental disease. These bouts are so much less often since I have received spiritual healing from the Lord and God. I rarely have them. I am so grateful for this. I believe that I have come a long way since my early years of recovery and the blessings from the Lord, God, Virgil and Angelica and other God-centered people who have made this happen. I truly pray this to happen to you.

This book is dedicated to readers who may have similar problems as I have and other illnesses and addiction. It is to inspire those who need hope. The idea of this book is solely through the inspiration of Virgil, Christ and God. Virgil stood by me while I was writing the text and suggested sentences and wording while I was writing them.

I also would like to dedicate this book to my mother, Mary Lou Harris. Throughout her life, she prayed and gave me the inspiration to get well. I have never known of a mother such as her. She shared love, strength, hope, and encouragement. She gave a lot to me. No one has ever supplied my needs more than my mother has. I hope everyone has enjoyed their mothers as much as I have mine. All of her living days, she was there for me. We pray for each other daily. Mother's prayers are special. It is said that a Mother's prayers bring spirituality and health to the soul of their child more than any other types of prayers.

This book is all about faith; faith within and faith without. After many episodes of mental illness it brings with it the fear of relapse into alcohol. I finally gave up and surrendered with faithful actions such as getting up and going on days when I felt bad and thought I would die to get well. Prayer, meditation, and completely giving my mind over to God forced me into believing that I was okay. God was in charge of my mental state.

Finally, it was as if I was charged with the gift of God's inspiration. I was trying to help others, twenty-four hours a day and seven days a week. I wanted to get well so bad. I would pray for healing, I would try to speak words of healing to others; I would put my all into healing of the sick.

I really meant what I said, "I will do anything and everything I can for God and Christ, because they gave me new life." A new life they gave me, and they have repaid me hundredfold. I only hope this small token of literature will be taken as a gift given back to God and Christ, for all they have done for me, and for all others in need of hope and inspiration to keep their lives glowing. May God continue with his blessings!

2015 I love my life and my wonderful friends

"Serenity Prayer"

God grant me the serenity to accept the things I cannot change, the courage to change the things I can and the wisdom to know the difference, living one day at a time, enjoying one moment at a time, accepting hardship as a pathway to peace, taking as Jesus did this sinful world as it is not as I would have it, trusting that You will make all things right if I surrender to Your will so that I may be reasonably happy in this life and supremely happy with You forever in the next.

Amen.

Reinhold Niebuhr

9 781478 762164